<u>Songbird</u>

Shauna McNamara

For Kaysha Ross,
My Songbird

TABLE OF CONTENTS

Acknowledgments

I was inspired to write this book because of the love I have for all of my grandchildren. I want them and everyone who reads this story to know that when you are faced with life's challenges always turn to God. He will help you make the right decisions. Trust him and don't allow anyone to change your mind!

To Ms. Lora Troutman and Ms. Rhea Edmonds, thank you for always pushing me to write more and share my story. May God continue to Bless you and The Peace and Freedom Committee.

Thank you, Grant Sykes, for your amazing illustrations that bring the characters to life. My appreciation goes out to Stephanie R. Bridges for your time and vision in bringing this book to fruition.

The proceeds from this book will support The Peace and Freedom Committee, a non-profit 501c3 organization. The mission of The Peace and Freedom Committee is "To promote racial equity by empowering, educating, and fostering understanding of the diverse cultures, backgrounds, and experience within Marion to build stronger, thriving communities."

"The purpose of education is to educate each one of us to think critically and to think intensively."
– Martin Luther King, Jr.

– one –
PRESSED FOR PEACE

*O*nce upon a time, there was a nice young lady named Kaysha Ross who went to visit Grannie every summer in Marion, Ohio. While visiting, Grannie would take her to church and choir practice. Right next door there lived a young man named Quincy; everybody called him Q. He was around her age, and his mom took him to choir practice too. That's how they met. At the time, they were both in middle school.

Years later, they got to know each other better when Kaysha's mom moved them to Marion, Ohio. When Kaysha visited Grannie, she hung out with Q. By this time, they were both attending Harding High School. Q showed her around, and they became close friends. Kaysha decided to join their high school choir. Q was also in the choir until he had to choose between singing and playing basketball. He chose basketball.

Kaysha continued to sing and one day it was announced that there was going to be a talent show. She asked Q to sing a song with her. He agreed, and they won the talent show! Everyone talked about how good they were. So much so, that one day Q's friend Rick came to them and said, "Let's all sing together at a house party."

Q was hesitant because the house party was on the west side. "Rick, you know we don't hang over there."

Rick responded, "Man, we play basketball over there during the tournament. What's the difference?"

"No, the tournament is in Lincoln Park. That's in between the west and east side," Q quickly retorted.

"Well, my friend Press is from the west side, and he is the one having the party, so we won't have anything to worry about."

Q, interrupted Rick, "Besides we don't even have a group. We haven't even practiced. Kaysha and I were just in one talented show!"

"The party is this weekend," Rick looked around at his friends. "We can all sing, so let's just sing this weekend." He had their attention. "There's going to be a concert and contest in four weeks at the Popcorn Festival. That's when we need to be ready to rock steady, and that's plenty of time for us to rehearse." Rick, excitedly added, "We could win $600.00. That's $200.00 apiece. Let's do this!" The three friends agreed.

That weekend they went to the house party on the west side, sang, and checked out the competition. Afterward, everyone came up to them and said you guys should be in the Popcorn Festival Contest. You all were amazing tonight.

Q looked at his friends, "What do you think Kaysha? Should we go for it?"

Rick nodding his head reminded them, "Yes, we could win $600."

Kaysha smiled and excitedly interjected, "What song should we sing?"

Press said, "*Wake Up Everybody* by Harold Melvin and the Blue Notes. There's a message in that song that the east and west side need to hear. Oh!" Press continued, "You should come up with a name for the group."

They thought it over. "I got it!" exclaimed Rick. "How about, KQR Trio?" That was the beginning of their exciting musical journey.

- two -
WRITING WRONGS

It was a nice weekend in Lincoln Park. Everyone had a good time watching the basketball tournament, eating BBQ, dancing, and listening to the live music which included the sounds of the KQR Trio. It was three weeks before the big performance and everyone was becoming good friends and started doing things together. The east side and west side went from sworn enemies to enjoying a friendly rivalry. People had house parties, skating parties, and BBQs all leading up to the main event.

During the week Rick and Press met up with Kaysha and Q. They had been working on a new song that Rick had written, adding adlibs and perfecting harmonies. They all agreed this weekend would be the perfect time to roll out their new jam, *The Hope and Peace Song*, and test it in front of a crowd before the big day.

After practice, Press said, "See what we can do when the east side and west side work together. Great things happen!"

That Saturday they went to the BBQ and rocked the park! Q and Kaysha sang lead, so people kept coming up to them telling them how great they sounded together and asking which one of them wrote the song. "Rick wrote the song," Kaysha and Q said on repeat.

"Wow, what, Rick wrote that?" was the response they got. Rick finally got his props.

Everything was going great and every performance was getting better and better. Then the Saturday before the Marion Popcorn Festival and the big performance, a fight broke out at the house party where they were singing. Q jumped in to break up the fight. He broke his leg and wrist during the brawl. Q was so upset about the fight that he told them he was done.

His friends looked at him in shock, but Press, Rick, and Kaysha understood. It was pretty messed up that he ended up getting hurt. However, Press reminded them that the contest was only one week away, and Q could probably use that $200 now more than ever.

- three -
TAKING THE LEAD

Now, it was Rick's turn to step up and sing lead at the Popcorn Festival. Kaysha and Rick only had a few rehearsals before the big day. They practiced together every day after school until they were ready. Then the big day arrived; the MC introduced them, "Now, coming to the stage, your favorite and mine, KQR Trio!" A confused rumble came from the crowd when only two people came to the stage. Even the MC was a little hesitant to walk off the stage, still waiting for Q with the golden voice.

Kaysha and Rick took their places, signaling to the crowd and the MC that tonight it would be a duo, and they *sang* that song. It sounded even better than when they first performed, *The Hope and Peace Song.* After what took place last week the meaning behind the lyrics made a huge impact on the crowd. After the last note, Rick and Kaysha grabbed hands and took a bow. When they looked up, they saw Q in the audience in a wheelchair cheering them on.

The crowd was pumped up, and started chanting, "Encore! Encore! We want one more!" So Rick did a solo and dedicated it to his friend Q. He sang a song to remind everyone how we all should stick together because you never know who you may need.

The first night at the festival went so well, that a producer, Mr. Clark, who was in the crowd took notice. He really liked the group and their positive message. He asked if they would open for a major recording artist the next night. Again, they rocked the crowd.

After that show, Mr. Clark told them he would like to meet with all three of them. He had heard all of them perform together before Q got hurt, and he admired how they all came together in a time of crisis. "Here is my card. Call me when Q gets better. I would like to meet with the KQR Trio to work out a recording contract."

– four –
RICK, IT'S YOUR MOVE

Several months went by, and Q's wrist and leg were getting better, doing his therapy three times a week. He felt bad about how he had left things with his friends. He reached out to Rick to find out how things were going with the group. Rick said that things were going well. He then asked, "Q, how is your recovery going, man? Everyone is asking if you're coming back to the group. I know math was never your strongest subject, but you do know we're not a trio without you."

Q chuckled, "Funny you should ask. I've been missing the music and I think you're right. My injuries are all healed and they haven't affected me playing basketball. Don't tell anyone this, but I really miss being on stage and singing in front of a crowd." Q then asked, "How are things with Kaysha?"

"Great, but I wanted to ask you something," Rick continued hesitantly, "Is there anything going on between you and Kaysha?"

"No, not at all. Why?"

Rick cleared his throat, "I would like to ask her out."

"Go for it!" Q said enthusiastically. He only saw Kaysha as a friend since they were kids and she used to come to Marion for Summers and stay with Grannie.

But little did he know Kaysha had eyes for him. Q and Kaysha spent a lot of time together practicing and singing before he got hurt. She had a crush on him since middle school and once she moved to Marion, went to school, and sang with Q her feelings only grew stronger.

After clearing things with Q, Rick finally got up enough nerve to ask her out one day after school.

"No, I'm sorry, Rick." Kaysha explained, "I am already seeing someone."

– five –
Kaysha's Prayer

When Q came back to rehearsal, Kaysha was happy to see him. They were laughing and talking. Kaysha asked Q how he was doing and if he was ready to sing again. Grabbing both her hands he answered, "Yes, let's do this!" After rehearsal, Kaysha asked Q if he would like to come over to catch up on some of the songs that she and Rick had been practicing. "Sure," Q was glad their friendship hadn't missed a beat. Kaysha and Q worked on the songs for a few weeks - just the two of them. They were getting close to performing as a trio again.

The producer from the Popcorn Festival called and asked if they could all talk. They met up and he asked if they could come to New York for the weekend. Mr. Clark held his hands up like a picture frame for them all to see, "I'll put you up in a hotel, you'll perform before packed crowds and eat at the best restaurants just like the stars

- all expenses paid." They all excitedly agreed. Kaysha thought New York would be the perfect place to let Q know how she felt about him. They went home and told their parents the amazing news.

The following week, they got all packed and met at the airport. The three of them took a shuttle to the hotel, but when they arrived Q had a lady friend waiting for him out front. The two of them embraced; Kaysha was crushed. She went to the front desk, checked herself in, and went straight to her room. Q turned around to introduce her, but Kaysha was gone. Later that evening when they all got together to rehearse, she kept messing up and no one understood why. Q and Rick looked at each other annoyed; they did not understand what was going on. "Let's call it a night and pick up in the morning," Rick suggested.

On the way down the hall, Rick's room was first. They all said good night, and Kaysha and Q kept walking toward their rooms in silence until Kaysha blurted out, "Why didn't you tell me you were seeing someone?"

"Because I'm not," Q responded.

"Oh, *really*?" Kaysha's voice was getting louder and her expressions got more animated, "Then who exactly was the lady you were hugging when we arrived?"

"That is my cousin. You rudely stormed off before I could introduce you. Besides, I thought you were seeing Rick."

"What? Who said that?"

"Rick told me." They both stared at each other bewildered. Q continued, "Well, he said he was going to ask you out. So..."

"He did ask me out, but I told him no because I was seeing someone." Kaysha's voice got quiet, and she looked into Q's eyes, "That someone is you."

Q scrunched his face in disbelief, "What? I told him we weren't seeing each other. So he had my blessing to proceed."

Kaysha continued, "I've had my eyes on you for a long time."

"I'm sorry. I didn't know, but I am not into dating, Kaysha. I am saving myself for my future wife. I am waiting for the right girl. But we can still be friends. I don't want to mix business with pleasure." Q, smiled warmly, "Are we still cool?"

"Yes," was all Kaysha could get out as she rushed past Q down the hallway to her room.

Kaysha was crushed by what Q said. She closed the door behind her and cried. She got on her knees and prayed, *Lord help clear my mind, dry my tears, and take the hurt away, so I can use the gift that You gave me.*

CHILDREN'S CHOIR

HOUSE PARTY!

THE BIG NIGHT

NEW YORK
NEW YORK

CHURCH DATE

WE DID IT!

— *six* —
DEAL OR NO DEAL

Kaysha went to sleep, and they all had breakfast together the next morning. That day rehearsal was better than usual. There were high-fives all around! Q's cousin, Shauna, came to the rehearsal, and afterward, they went sightseeing. Kaysha, Q, and Rick loved being in the big city. It was such a mindblowing departure from what they were used to in Marion.

Later they all got ready for the concert, and as usual, the KQR Trio rocked the house! After the show, they all went out to dinner. They laughed and reminisced about how the group got started at the basketball court in Lincoln Park, jamming at BBQ cook-offs, and the big show at the Popcorn Festival. They only wished Press could have been there.

The following day they met up with Mr. Clark. He could not contain his excitement, "You all were amazing! It was like you have been performing on big stages for years. The crowd could feel the chemistry! I want to offer you a recording contract!" The friends all just looked at each other and smiled.

The next day would be their last performing and hanging out in New York. They did two shows; one in the afternoon and one that night. They had a blast, got some food from a street vendor, and headed back to their rooms. They had to get up early for their flight back to Marion. Kaysha thanked God for such an amazing experience and fell asleep wondering if she would become a star.

The next morning the producer stopped them in the hotel lobby, "I love what you three did this weekend. You rocked every show! I'd like to offer you a contract to sign with me exclusively!" Again the kids were quiet.

They all looked at each other and took a deep breath. Finally, Q spoke up, "We must talk it over with our parents."

Mr. Clark nodded his head, "Yes, of course. That's to be expected because you would need their permission to drop out of high school and be tutored on the road." They all looked at each other in disbelief.

This was a big decision. They rode to the airport, checked in, and got on their flight. When they got settled in their seats, Rick broke the long silence, "How do y'all feel?"

Q said, "Man, I did not see that coming. Drop out of school to pursue this dream of singing?" He shook his head, "That was never on my radar. I have a chance to play basketball. Singing is just something I did because everyone else said I have a golden voice."

Kaysha chimed in, "I love to sing but dropping out of school and being tutored on the road between rehearsal and performances is a bit much. I want to become a nurse."

"What about you?" Q and Kaysha asked in unison.

"School is too important. Once you have your diploma no one can take it from you. Singing only lasts for so long for most people. I am torn. I know what my mind is telling me, but my gut is telling me something totally different."

On the other hand, Mr. Clark was fired up about finding the next big sensation. He was ready to get busy putting together their wardrobe and having photo shoots so they could look like a top-tier group! He was thinking about lining up their next gigs, getting their shoe sizes, and finding out what colors and hairstyles they preferred.

Kaysha, Q, and Rick all went home feeling confused. The excitement of the trip turned sad as they realized this was more than just singing. This was a life-changing decision they were faced with. What will Q do? What will Kaysha do? What will Rick do?

– seven –
Second Chances

It was a nice sunshiny morning with crisp air. The KQR Trio were headed back to school and their regular routines. Kaysha welcomed the normalcy. At the breakfast table, Kaysha's parents asked her about the trip to New York. Her smile dropped, "I am running late. Can we talk about it at dinner?"

Q's parents asked him the same question. He mumbled, "Okay."

His mother asked, "How was your cousin, Shauna?"

"She met us at the hotel when we arrived, and we went sightseeing the next day. It was good to see her and catch up."

Q's dad was intrigued by the idea of them performing in New York. It was a big deal and he wanted to hear the details. "*Well* tell us about the trip," he gestured his hand in a circular motion requesting more.

"Can we talk about it tonight at dinner?" Q's mom and dad both gave him a stern look and then his dad threw up his hands in surrender, "Sure, I need to get to work. See you both tonight."

When Rick came downstairs for breakfast his dad was already gone. He had to be at work early. His mom smiled brightly when she saw him, "Good morning. Breakfast is ready, son." Rick sat down and began to eat. "How was the trip?" Rick couldn't contain himself. He told her everything about the rehearsals, sightseeing, restaurants, performances, and the contract offer.

Rick's mother took in all the information and responded, "All I am going to say, Son, is this is your life. You must make up your own mind."

He leaned over and kissed her on the cheek and said, "Thanks, Mom."

"Have a beautiful and blessed day. We'll talk more this evening when your father is home."

"Okay, I will see you tonight. You have a blessed day too."

Kaysha, Rick, and Q met up at school. They all had senior lunch at the same time. They talked and each one agreed they could not quit school. Their minds were made up.

After lunch on the way to their next class, Rick asked Kaysha to go to the school's bonfire that Friday. Kaysha was happy that Rick was still interested in hanging out with her after how she responded when he first asked her out. "Yes," she replied with a big grin. Q overheard them making plans.

That evening Q and Kaysha went home and talked to their parents. They told them about how great the trip was and what Mr. Clark had proposed; it got quiet. Kaysha told her parents she was going to stay in school. Q told his parents that the group discussed it, and they all decided to stay in school. Their parents were proud of their decision.

Mr. Clark was not giving up that easily though. He kept calling trying to change their minds. It reached a point where Q's dad told him, "Please stop calling! We cannot entertain this until school is out. My son has a chance to play pro basketball."

Kaysha's dad hung up on Mr. Clark after telling him, "For the last time, wait until school is out, then we can talk!"

Rick and his parents invited Mr. Clark over. They wanted to hear more about his offer. They all sat at the kitchen table and listened to Mr. Clark. It was very enticing. He turned to Rick, "I want the whole trio. Please talk to Kaysha and Q. But if they cannot be convinced, I will sign you and build a new trio around you. We can make a lot of money. This is a chance of a lifetime!" Rick listened intently, but he already knew it was a no-go. His friends were adamant about staying in school, and he was not going to abandon them to form a new group. Besides, Rick was more excited about his big date with Kaysha on Friday. He wasn't going to let anybody mess that up.

– *eight* –
FRIEND ZONED

Kaysha and Rick met at the bonfire. They talked and got to know each other outside of singing. They had a nice time walking around, listening to music, laughing, and sharing their dreams for the future. It was time to say goodbye, so Rick escorted her home and tried to kiss her. Kaysha pulled away and instead hugged him at the end of their date.

Rick asked Kaysha to go to the movies the following Friday. They had a great time. After escorting her home, he tried to kiss her. Again, Kaysha pulled away. He got the message. She asked Rick to go to church with her on Sunday. He said yes and did not try to kiss her again. The next Friday Rick and Kaysha went to Q's basketball game. After the game he took her home. This time he reached out for a hug. They enjoyed one another's company, but Rick was starting to think they were just friends. Despite wanting more, that was ok with him because Kaysha was so much fun to hang out with.

Press was having a BBQ. He called Kaysha, Q, and Rick to come and sing at the party. Q was hesitant about going back to the west side but he finally agreed. It was important to show solidarity and not go backward.

During the party, Rick and Kaysha went out by the pool. Q noticed Kaysha and Rick had been hanging out for a while. Q signaled for Rick to come over and speak to him. He began, "So, Rick my man, how is dating Kaysha going?"

Rick shook his head, "Man, she's a good girl. Not at all like the others I've dated in the past. We laugh, talk, just have a good time. Listen, we've been on four dates now, and I still haven't even kissed her."

"What man, *really*?" Q responded intrigued.

"Get this, I even went to church with her and had dinner at her parent's house. We even pray together. It's different," Rick smiled and added, "But I like it."

Based on Rick's response, Q thought maybe Kaysha was still into him. He went back and forth about what he should do about his feelings for her. After a lot of consideration, Q caught up with Kaysha before school and asked her out. She could not believe her ears.

"Wait, what? I thought you weren't into dating. Remember, you don't mix business with pleasure. You were saving yourself for your future wife..." Kaysha had more.

But Q held up his hands, "Wait wait, let me explain. I know what I said but I have been thinking about how much I hurt you."

Kaysha jumped in, "Yes in the beginning I was hurt. I had a crush on you for a long time. But I prayed about it, and now I am better and stronger!" Q tried to get a word in, but Kaysha interrupted, "Besides, I am seeing Rick now, and we are getting along great. I like him, he is respectful and kind; he treats me well and we laugh *and* pray together. Q had heard enough. He knew he should just throw in the towel for the sake of his friendships. But before he could bow out gracefully, out of nowhere Rick walked up and Kaysha planted a kiss on his cheek and sashayed away.

"Wow," Q and Rick were both in shock.

Rick was excited about the kiss from Kaysha but also confused because it came out of nowhere. Rick questioned, "What were the two of you talking about?" Q just stood there dumbfounded and then walked away. He experienced a feeling of emptiness that he had never felt before. He thought to himself, *I let my songbird get away.*

After 3rd period class, Q saw Kaysha in the hallway by her locker. Q begged, "Kaysha, please can we talk?"

In a sharp tone, Kaysha asked, "What now Q?"

"Not, here. Can I stop by your house after school?

Kaysha shook her head in disbelief. But she could empathize with how he felt, and they were still friends. "Okay, come by my house after school."

Q was relieved, "Okay, I will be over after basketball practice."

The day went on and the three of them ate lunch together. Rick noticed they were not talking to one another. He questioned, "What is going on between you two?"

They responded in unison, "Nothing!"

- nine -
Q SHOOTS HIS SHOT

School let out. Q went to basketball practice, but he couldn't get Kaysha off his mind, so he asked the coach if he could leave early. He needed to talk to her. When he arrived, Kaysha and Q went outside to sit on the back patio. Her mom asked if they would like to have some lemonade. "Yes, please," Q said. He could already feel his throat getting dry.

Kaysha turned to Q, "What else is there to talk about?"

"Kaysha, please hear me out. I am so sorry for hurting you. I did not mean to. I wrongfully prejudged you and I regret that. Kaysha nodded her head but remained quiet. "I thought you were footloose and fancy-free. I thought you were with a bunch of different guys; I am so sorry!"

"What would make you think that? Q, you've known me forever."

"I know. I know, and I should have judged you by your character and who I know you to be. But Kaysha you have to admit, you are super popular. You're a cheerleader, on the debate team, a reporter for the school newspaper, in the choir, and a part of the band! You are always talking to different guys."

"That is my job, Q. I have to interview different people, practice with the debate team and perform. You know firsthand I am always about my business. None of what you're saying adds up to me seeing any of these guys. I'm disappointed that you saw me that way." Q could tell Kaysha was beginning to get upset.

Q grabbed Kaysha's hand, "You sing like a songbird. When you sing you get all in those guys' faces."

Kaysha, jerked her hand away, "Q that is because I know how to work a song. When you perform, you are all up in the ladies' faces, right Golden Voice?" Q did not have a comeback. Kaysha continued, "I was in your face but you did not take *that* personally! I really liked you, Q. It was more than just a friendship for me. But you shut me down, and I moved on! It's too late. Don't you get it? I am seeing Rick now."

"I am sorry. Kaysha, I really like you; I cannot stop thinking about you. Q kissed Kaysha on the lips and her heart skipped a beat.

She pushed him away frustrated. "Why now Q?"

"I now know you are not easy and don't put out like other girls. Kaysha, I have been waiting all my life for a girl like you."

A tear rolled down her cheek. Q gently wiped it away. Kaysha looked into Q's eyes and spoke, "I am sorry. I want to be with Rick."

"I know but if it doesn't work out, I am here. Can I give you one last kiss to say goodbye?"

Kaysha said, "Yes." Just then, they heard the tray of lemonade crashing and glass shattering on the concrete. They turned to see Rick looking at them both in disbelief.

Kaysha's mother rushed out, and all four of them quietly tried to pick up the shattered pieces.

− Ten −

BREAK UP TO MAKE UP

After Kaysha's mom went back inside, Rick got in Q's face, "What the heck is going on, Man? I thought we were cool."

Kaysha got in between her two best friends. "Wait, nothing's going on."

Rick moved Kaysha out of the way. "Q what's up with you kissing my girl?"

Q shook his head, "I'm sorry man. She's into you."

"It doesn't look like it! This is messed up man. I asked you in the beginning if there was anything between you and Kaysha before I started dating her." Q hung his head and allowed him to continue, "You told me no, go for it. Now look! You go and do this behind my back. Unbelievable!"

"Man, I am sorry. At first, I didn't think she was

the right girl for me. I attempted to hold my feelings back. Listen, Rick, as much as I tried, she doesn't want to be with me." Q turned and looked at Kaysha before continuing, "Kaysha wants to be with you. I'm sorry."

"Q, please just leave." Kaysha turned her back to him. Q left knowing he had hurt his two best friends.

Rick was still upset. "Kaysha, why were you and Q kissing? You still have never given me a chance to kiss you. I just don't understand. Do you have feelings for him? Be honest."

"No, I promise. We were just saying goodbye to what might have been. I have imagined myself being with him since sixth grade."

"Do you always kiss him goodbye?

"No today was the first time. I had strong feelings for him for a long time. But I know now he is not the one for me. God showed me that when we were in New York.

Kaysha reached out for Rick's hand but he stood with his hands down by his side. "He was not into me until you and I started seeing each other, and he really misjudged my character. I am sorry. You should not have seen that. It was never going to happen again. I told him over and over again that I wanted to be with you, Rick. Kaysha's voice started to crack and she could feel the tears coming, "I cannot do this anymore, maybe we should just be friends."

Kaysha began to walk back into the house, but Rick spun her around, "A kiss between old friends does not change how I feel about you." Kaysha and Rick hugged, talked, and drank the lemonade her mom brought back outside for just the two of them.

Before Rick left for the evening, Kaysha asked, "What about the group?"

"It's a wrap for the trio. I choose you. We must go our separate ways. From here on out it's just the two of us. Unless you want to be with Q."

"No, I want to be with you, Rick." Kaysha and Rick shared their first kiss.

The next day at school, Kaysha and Rick met Q at lunch to tell him the group was over.

"You two do not have to do this."

Rick asked Q, "Will you respect our relationship?"

"Yes, 100%. We have come a very long way as friends and as a group. Just like the east side and west side, I do not want there to be any beef between the KQR Trio. That would be like going backward."

Rick thought about it. "You're right. We've come too far as a group and community." They shook hands and fist-bumped.

Q turned to Kaysha, "Again, I'm sorry for everything."

"Okay Q. We are cool," Kaysha was happy everything was resolved. "Bring it in guys." The three friends hugged. Later that week, Press asked the trio if they would sing at the city-wide senior graduation party in a couple of weeks.

They all graduated from H.S. that June. Mr. Clark still mourned the group that got away.

Press was impressed that the east side and west side maintained their friendly rivalry. Kaysha became a nurse, Q went to college and was offered a chance to play pro basketball, and Rick took a job with Mr. Clark scouting for new talent.

Before they all went their separate ways, KQR Trio rocked Lincoln Park one last time. They sang *Wake Up Everybody* by Harold Melvin and the Blue Notes and *The Hope and Peace Song* by Richard "Rick" Thomason, and Press had a special request, *Back Together Again* by Roberta Flack and Donny Hathaway. It was the best community concert Marion had ever seen!

The moral of the story is: be honest about your feelings, be respectful of other people's choices, and don't be judgemental towards anyone. We are all God's children. So, let's learn to follow the golden rule and treat each other the way we want to be treated so no one gets hurt.